T0129136

Cool Blue EMOTION

Rhymes & Reason

PHIL FORD

authorHOUSE®

AuthorHouse™
1663 Liberty Drive
Bloomington, IN 47403
www.authorhouse.com
Phone: 1 (800) 839-8640

Published by AuthorHouse   05/25/2017

ISBN: 978-1-5246-9356-5 (sc)
ISBN: 978-1-5246-9355-8 (e)

Library of Congress Control Number: 2017908169

Print information available on the last page.

Scripture taken from the King James Version of the Bible.

Table of Contents

Worthy Birth

Do these words exist elsewhere too?
I hope so; and they're held as true.
I would cry if they held no worth,
For I was there, during their birth.

1

SLEEP

Has anyone truly
analyzed our sleep?
Some rock to and fro -
the mattress beneath.
Caught in a dream world;
reality strains.
An uncontrolled time;
our subconscious reigns.

Some sleep-in just to
avoid the real world.
Some sleep-in for a
natural unfurl.
Sleep itself can be
a welcome reward,
for those who have spent
the day with the sword.

MUSIC

There's an excitement that reverberates
on the drums of man.
Movement purely offered to generate
thought across the land.
The genre of thought is as various
as the notes themselves.
Relaxing stillness to vicarious
feelings to be held.

There's excitement that causes interest
in the pains of man.
Directly, or through subtle inference,
one sees one must stand.
Emotions brought out of pure tones and notes
exhaust and relieve,
so mankind can open up to new hope;
listen and believe.

Such News to a Friend

I spoke to a close friend about her love.
There's a real problem with this;
I upset her bliss.
I didn't know the two shared any love.

She assured me, "You did me a favor."
She said, "I was too involved."
Wow; what have I solved?
One cannot fine tune love with a saber.

So what if he was seen with another?
It's been several months back –
I can't be exact.
Could have been a friend, not a new lover.

If I lose my friend from this debacle,
I'll count it an awesome loss.
Whatever the cost,
I must restore her trust and her laughter.

A gem of advice for those who would talk
about one to another.
Hold your tongue brother!
Friendship saved could be of valuable stock.

Fortunes of War

Me.
My job.
I'm happy.
There are good times.
But, I'll not be bought!
What happened to fairness?
Can there be no agreement?
Will they soon find a common ground?
When can my life quit turning around?
I must retain my personal respect.
I'll try to cooperate and do my best.
Has communicating been replaced by facades?
Are the fortunes of war worth the terrible battle?
I want to find an answer other than my resignation.
The fate of an idealist is certain unless others believe.
I suppose many wish I would succumb to their preconceptions.
I'm not a rebel, but I must be true to my conscious and my ideals.
I pray for a rebirth of the essence of Integrity – Idealism.
Soon, I'm sure, the day will arrive when I will be forced to make known my decision,
I'll decide.
I will.
Me.

THE PLEASANT LABOR

What about the guy who uses a pen?
Why does he care about thoughts from within?
Put it on paper,
the heart will savor;
the pleasant labor.

He's not quite like the average earthling.
Not a bit better than any he's seen.
Put it on paper,
the heart will savor;
the pleasant labor.

His friends know portions of him very well.
He doesn't conceal those thoughts that he's felt.
Put it on paper,
the heart will savor;
the pleasant labor.

Never pushing that his work shows talent.
Allows his soul its true quest for balance.
Put it on paper,
the heart will savor;
the pleasant labor.

DREAMS

Fantasies are said to be wasting time.
But the strength they give fights criticism.
Life would be unbearable without mine.
Life is hued by dreams.

To have peace about things to come
is based on faith in times not yet produced.
Whether you're a banker or a bum.
Life is hued by dreams.

Let us set goals so forward we can march
towards that which excites from within.
But our lives may wither from too much starch!
Life is hued by dreams.

THE ROYAL WEDDING

Why is it that the poor in flesh are to
be healed by the feeding of their spirits?
I can't see why some feel that the millions
spent help the poor who cannot get near it!
Tell me, when was the last time the poor drank
from a five-figure bowl? They'll not see it!
Feeding the poor?

Was it a time of love shrouded over
by costly pageantry and tradition?
Or was it, as they said, a shot in the
arm for the riot ridden conditions?
I'm dumbfounded to how tempers were eased
by the show of six-figure explosions.
Employing the unemployed?

How many single parent families
made ends meet more easily based on this?
How were the parentless human beings
aided in their unhopeful search for bliss?
To this mockery, hearing any phrase
other than 'Hail Caesar' would be amiss.
Caring for the widows and the orphans?

LIFE

Some folks here said that this life is a maze.
Some have their bearings; some are in a daze.
I believe the choice of goals set the pace
to whether we're at ease or caused to race.

What's the secret to keeping peace of mind?
From where is the strength that keeps us in line?
A source outside ourselves is the one way
to reach our goals and to thrive day by day.

I'll not apologize for my life's source.
One who navigates and nurtures my course.
The source that protects from life's acid rain.
The One I speak of? Jesus is His name.

The Life of Friendships

How do friendships maintain themselves
when acreage breaks the tied binds?
Is the essence of the feeling
severed with location goodbyes?

Must we always find that we're not
remembered by those left behind?
Or, are there those who will neglect
the distance and maintain the find?

I will tell you one of my thoughts
to answer doubts of a friend's worth.
Friends of true measure won't accept
time's bid against true friendships' birth.

PATIENCE

There aren't too many people in the world
who have attained the virtue of patience.
Fact is, if most earthlings titled their lives,
the header would read 'off to the races.'

What can be earned from a life not filled with
active confusion and thought collision?
What can be learned from taking time to breathe
during this life, in between decisions?

BREAKDOWN

There's a friend I met not too long ago
whose had problems with the life that he knows.
The friend wanted to talk about his life
and explain to me the source of his strife.

Not more than a year ago, he began,
I was working nearly hand over hand.
My full-time job, my part-time job, and more;
my wife, and I have two sons I adore.

Pressures of father, lover, provider,
were more than my skills could always cover.
But there was a voice inside my own mind
that urged me to maintain and not to whine.

One evening while traveling home from work,
deep within my chest I began to hurt.
Very unlike any feeling before;
unstable and lost, I could drive no more.

As I walked towards home, I became lost.
The thoughts inside my head endlessly tossed.
Where is my house? Where is my family?
I had to sit down; my feet were too free.

It took me eight months to reach this resolve.
It's hard to explain what all it involved.
The doctors called it a complete breakdown;
I'm thankful that my wife is still around.

My friend, he said to me, here's some advice.
Take it and keep it; don't put it on ice.
Don't build yourself a hand over hand life;
accept only love and reject the strife.

RESIGNATION DATE

Well, the time has come;
a new note to strum.
My choice has been made –
resignation date.

An exciting move;
a new chosen groove.
Excitement now great –
resignation date.

A new position;
one of decision.
Better now than late –
resignation date.

Sadness leaving friends;
new ones to begin.
True friends always stay –
resignation date.

THE SEA

How the Sun softly dances through the sky;
chasing the horizon to where it hides.
The clouds collide, floating above.
Most of all, it's the sea I love.

Baby turtles crawling across the sand.
Residue between my toes from the land.
This particular walkway lends to the peace
as it travels to the sea and beneath.

Ancient looking coral formations rise
up from their birth to lightly touch the sky.
Accenting each – the Sun, the sea and the sand –
Their rocky existence in quiet command.

CONFLICT

Narrow-minded words?
Your vision is blurred.
Not a kind thought heard.
Conflict.

Speaking only hate.
A difference to state.
Time to clean the slate?
Conflict

Is it good to fight
when you know you're right?
Understanding slight.
Conflict.

You know who's the boss.
Maybe take the loss.
Chiseled or embossed?
Conflict.

PERCEPTION

The way I see it,
you don't see it at all.
Or, is it that you
see, but still you stall?
I'm confident of
the situation;
why do you still need
an explanation?

The way I heard it
was that she walked out.
But you disagree
and you're snowed with doubt.
Fact is that neither
one saw conception;
so we must lean on
our own perceptions.

THE GAME

The business world
has its own rules set.
All of the rules must
be followed and kept.
Don't step on toes by
breaking one's façade.
Not wearing three-piece?
You'll be labeled odd.

Who do you know and
who can you contact?
If it's no one then
you'll get the subtract.
They'll need to be rich
or have some power
to allow you to
seek and devour.

The business world
can be fair to all
if the team players
in fairness don't balk.
The qualities aren't
unfair in themselves;
as long as the game,
not fairness, is shelved.

THE CHIP

What is there to gain
from standing alone?
They're against the grain,
those seeds you have sown.

Shooting from the hip;
we spoke of that once.
But what of the chip
you've covered for months?

Suppose it gets bumped
by the force of two?
Will you stand or run?
What will the chip do?

It must be lonely
protecting the chip.
Kindness too boldly
might cause it to slip.

Then what do you do
with no protector?
You'll find when he's through;
the real defector.

Friday

The Sun
tries so hard
to do
its own part.
Making
the day grand
to sit
or to stand.
Feelings
learn to hope –
Today
I can cope
with all
that comes up
from morn
until sup.
The end
of the week
makes joy
start to speak
of peace
soon to come
from rest –
Friday's done.

THE FULLNESS OF LIFE

From day one, when our conception took place,
our short lives are often riddled with strife.
We can't make choices yet from womb space.
The fullness of life.

At an early age we learn about love.
When love's deprived, the effect is not slight.
But when it's shared freely as from above –
The fullness of life.

During the years of learning youth expands.
The joy of new love flies high like a kite.
Learning to cope – emotional demands.
The fullness of life.

After time has accumulated years,
your loving mate still desires your sight.
You'll find the shared laughter outweighs the tears.
The fullness of life.

Sweet Emotion

There comes a time
when one realizes the essence
of what the heart is truly about.
Not muscle,
nor flesh and blood;
but rather, the embodiment
of passionate emotion.
A level of emotion
that flows, absorbs, contains,
enables, frees, caresses, learns,
accompanies, represents and shares
more than thought or conversation.
This sought after level truly
encompasses sweet emotion.

Clouded Vision

I saw you in the mirror today;
a fear I've always had.
The day that I turned into you –
the look that made me sad.

The demons whisper in my ear,
louder than my clearest thought.
Impacting the way I look at life –
fighting battles I've already fought.

Heavy is my tired heart;
riddled with murky tears.
Not attempting to drift –
the pain of passing years.

I stand in the darkness;
faced with the current me.
Haunted by the vision
of whom I seem to be.

Where do I go from here?
To stay or just move on?
Thoughts remain unsettled –
yesterday and beyond.

VEILS

An opportunist
of sorts – choice facades;
moving through life as
an actor in a play.
What's the advantage
to these sort of odds?
Can it be true that
social crime does pay?

And now comes the brunt
of varied faces;
no one ever knows
he who wears the mask.
There must be many
such unknown spaces
deep within he who
in loneliness basks.

An Autumn Sonnet

What doth the wind know of my love?
Can the wind speak of the contentment when my love is near?
I think the wind knoweth not of my love.
What doth the sea know of my love?
Will the sea speak of the depth of my love's eyes?
I think the sea knoweth not of my love.
Will the Moon attempt to speak of my love?
To share the emotions of Olympus that fulfill the yearnings of the multitude.
Even so, the Moon falls short.
What can the weavings of the universe know of my love?
Demi I say; demi!
With the universe showing pale in its wisdom,
only one true value counts – my love itself.
Two spirits in kindred as one.

The Rooms of my Heart

The varied rooms of my small heart
are offered to those in my life
that I care for.
How they respond to my offer
determines how full my heart is
behind each door.

When the rooms in my human heart
are occupied by those who love,
there is a spark.
But, when a room is left vacant
or the offer sadly refused,
the room is dark.

Those who share their warm love with me
have built a mansion filled with rooms
around my soul.
Heaven's promise of a mansion
is mine to enjoy, even now,
to help me grow.

My life has been blessed because your
true love and prayers keep us close;
never apart.
Thank you for living here with me,
nestled in the decorated
rooms of my heart.

My Youth

I was there
in the beginning.
It was my beginning.

My time
was my comfort zone;
pushed hard for the end zone.

All was clear.
I knew the best way.
Things had to be my way.

Not alone,
but never to share.
Chose not to give my share.

People known
often slipped away.
Too often, pushed away.

Endless strength
unleashed by my youth.
My weakness was my youth.

THE LINE

You start out the morning, so it seems,
with human robots standing on teams.
Whether it is stove parts or light beams,
no one gets anxious, nobody steams.
The line moves on, buzzing like bees.

What happened to the grass and the trees;
to children playing and dogs with fleas;
to guitar strings and piano keys;
to social events; backyard parties?
The line moves on, buzzing like bees.

When the line's moving, no one's at ease.
No type of humor – no one will tease.
Always praying for hints of a breeze.
Expecting to see them brake and scream.
The line moves on, buzzing like bees.

Cool Blue Emotion

Stirring,
yet strangely without warmth.
Chilled brine
steeps the Primrose
from the azure Wisteria.
Cool blue emotion.

Steel-blue vapor
entices a temperamental mist.
Blindly imbued spirit
is fitfully teased
from the sapphire Hyacinth.
Cool blue emotion.

Hostile sensibilities
press with insolence.
They permeate all sensuous thought.
Tears flow
from the dismal Willow.
Cool blue emotion.

The impertinent passage of time.
The demonstrative stillness of movement.
Wringing with pain;
frigid from scars.
Cool blue emotion.

What About Their Lives

What about their years?
Have they had the time
to gain peace of mind?
What about their tears?

What about their past?
Does joy outweigh bad?
Have they become mad?
Will the anger last?

What about their age?
Have they seen the Sun?
Have they felt undone?
What about this stage?

What about their loves?
Was the passion real?
Did the sandman steal?
Please let them still love?

What about right now?
Can they share their grief?
Will they keep their beliefs?
To this end I vow.

TREASURE

Time is of the essence.
What is the essence of time?
Not enough of it –
too much on our hands.
We have all there is;
no more – no less.
Use it wisely.

Come With Me

I spread my wings as I fly through the air.
The cool spray from the sea moistens my hair.
I've chosen the sky; if you wish to share.
Come fly with me.

I stroke with my limbs; the current roles by.
During the baptism, I hear a sigh.
The waters are pleasant to those who'll try.
Come swim with me.

My lungs reach out for the fresh taste of the wind.
My legs feel the warmth of the life deep within.
My knees feel the strength of their flexing bends.
Come run with me.

I look towards the trees to see the small birds.
I focus my ears to the sounds that I've heard.
Aromas of greens and browns can be learned.
Come walk with me.

The new beat of my heart resounds with joy.
New fantasies within learn to be coy.
All of life's hues dance and say ahoy.
Come love with me.

Build and Mend

Lightning flashes on either side.
Is it in love or space I hide?
I dream of peace swelling within;
I love the space I've found with my friend.

New thoughts, better yet old that have grown.
How long ago those seeds were sown.
The trees of life grow strong with new bark.
Only true friendships bring light more than dark.

The joy of living could rapture the mind;
but pain and sorrow continue to whine.
I seek relief while I cherish a friend.
The strength of this continues to mend.

Sneering are the boundaries that limit these thoughts –
imposing their barriers as a fence so taught.
Reflections of a mirror that keep me in line,
urge me to search and not neglect the find.

I believe that all life builds from the old;
but only if the new will assist and unfold.
I believe that peace is a work of art;
so gather your materials and fill up your cart.

Save the Light

I saw a light,
a very new light,
as it flickered from its new beginning.
Unknown to me,
this light I did see,
from where it started and where it would end.
Yes this one,
who would go unsung,
began to strengthen to a steady flame.
But soon to leave,
and some would grieve,
for this new wine dying in the drain.
Where is the guilt
for this light just spilled?
I think it begins long before the start.
I pray that we
will finally see
no matter how slight, it's still a heart.

THE PRISON

The pictures in my mind of that cell
are frightening to me, more than Hell.
How long ago was that? I'm not sure;
but the horror of that place is pure.

I remember feeling cold and wet.
I still feel the chill of my own sweat.
The summer's heat, I hated it so,
for smothering me – time went so slow.

I slept very near a killer there.
He killed his son and beat his daughter.
What caused this man to become so mean?
One more year there and I would have been.

The guards were emotionless to a fault.
They would beat you, whip you, make you crawl;
no hesitation when causing blood;
just hoping you'd die from your red flood.

The years, they're good to help me forget
The cold, rotten mattress where I slept.
But I still feel the pain of that time;
and worse, I don't remember the crime.

SHIPWRECKED

It's been nine months since I left the port of Maine.
The echoes of my friends saying, "you're insane."
And insane I may be for I'm captive here,
all alone on this island where nothing is near.

My boat, now in pieces from the crashing waves,
was my only hope to be spotted and saved.
It rested on the reef whose coral did wait
to quench its life and endanger its weight.

The storm I had found caught the boat by its hull;
tossed and threw it until my senses were dull.
For six days I felt like a sardine in there,
being pressed and packed with seemingly no care.

And then that scream as from a giant white whale
came screeching through my ears, still trapped in my jail.
The hull was tearing – there could be no escape;
the knife of the sea destroying my drape.

My feet were then wet, but I was deathly afraid
to leave the doomed boat where I had become slave.
Unsure what took place after this fearful bout,
for my courage gave way and I then passed out.

I look back to when I awoke in my ship
seeing the torn floor where the coral reef ripped.
Hoping I was alive, but afraid to look
outside my torn ship where the great sea still lurked.

Yes, still alive, but shipwrecked here I regret.
No sign of another human since Maine I left.
I dream that someday I may be located
and end this nightmare for which I've been slated.

A SPECIAL WAY

(Song Lyric)

I see you, all the time.
Not with my eyes, but with my mind.
I touch you, all the time.
Not on your skin, but that inside.

Lady you're the one, the girl I've waited for.
And with you by my side, what man could ask for more?
And I wander what you think of me
as you go down life's way.
I want your heart to sing of me
in a very special way.

I hear you, as you cry.
Not with my ears, but with my eyes.
As you walk towards me, with your head held high,
I see you face; I feel your smile.

Lady you're the one, the girl I've waited for.
And with you by my side, what man could ask for more?
And I wander what you think of me
as you go down life's way.
I want your heart to sing of me
In a very special way.

THE NURSE

Who is this lady?
She moves through the halls as life through the heart.
I think that maybe
within the whole, she is a valued part.
Her white uniform
hints to distinction in some gained knowledge;
and if true to form,
will concentrate to see pain abolished.
Where has she come from?
Is there some school to teach people to care?
Can hearts, like the drum,
resound on command when it comes time to share?
I think she was born
into this world to do what can't be taught –
to help the worn
and to share strength with those who have naught.

THE CAPITAL

It's almost midnight.
His hair has been shaven; his last rites read.
Showing signs of fright,
but feeling calm – or so he has said.
Which one decided?
Who was blameless enough and free from guilt?
Must have confided;
It isn't known just how their lives were built.

How dim the lights are.
His life now smothered to pay for his crime.
Some guy in a bar,
'the kid deserved it, he's nothing but slime,'
The act was grotesque
that invited the judgement from his peers.
But who will protest
their humorous attitudes and their jeers.

Do we have the right?
Can we choose death for another human?
Did we show our might?
Will the violence stop its consuming?
And what happens next?
Are we now in line for our judgement?
And even at best,
were our actions true to our commitment?

THE BOSS IF ON VACATION

8:30 am	Where is my timecard?
8:45 am	It's so nice outside.
9:00 am	Have you seen my pen?
9:30 am	Well, I have to work.
10:15 am	Where has he gone to?
10:45 am	You have a message.
11:00 am	The sky is so clear.
11:35 am	How about some lunch?
11:45 am	I'll never get this done.
12:00 pm	Will you call him back?
12:10 pm	I'm going to lunch.
12:15 pm	Will you catch the phones?
12:30 pm	When will he be back?
12:40 pm	It's so nice outside.
12:45 pm	Have you gone to lunch?
1:30 pm	I'm so frustrated.
2:00 pm	Oh, what should we do?
2:45 pm	I want to go home.
3:30 pm	I just don't have the time.
4:30 pm	What about Florida?
5:00 pm	See you tomorrow…

QUESTIONS TO ANSWER

(Song Lyric)

What if I were to live in a cloud?
Would I enjoy life or become a shroud?
How hard would it be for me to exist;
created harmony like all of the rest?

I've got questions to answer
and my life to live.
I need someone to love all my life –
all my love… I will give.

The cloud of marriage now stands over me.
Will you be my mate through eternity?
Will you accept my love and release your own?
Invite our God to live in our home?

Time… it passed so slowly;
you're not by my side.
I need someone so I won't be lonely.
I want you here… by my side.

We've joined together to live now as one.
Begin to live the new life begun.
Answered my questions – completed my life;
by sharing my son and being my wife.

Time… it passed so quickly;
now our race is run.
We've shared our lives, our love and our sorrows;
Best of all… as one.

Fade Away

(Song Lyric)

Sunlight on my back
makes me feel so fine.
Travelin' along the countryside
to help me ease my mind.
The cares of the city seem to fade
away.
To another place;
to another day.

Way down the road, that's where I
want to be.
Let loose of my mental load – all
my thoughts set free.
No problems of tomorrow, no
problems of today.
The problems now before me soon
will fade away.

Moonlight in my eyes
makes me feel so calm.
Ridin' down this country road
and looking far beyond.
Nothing but starlight
as far as I can see.
Wonderin' who I am
and who I want to be.

Way down the road, that's where I
want to be.
Let loose of my mental load – all
my thoughts set free.
No problems of tomorrow, no
problems of today.
The problems now before me soon
will fade away.

Twilight in the air
makes the day worthwhile.
Goin' down the road –
all I do is smile.
Thinkin' I could be
the only one on Earth.
Ridin' on my bike –
takin' another curve.

Way down the road, that's where I
want to be.
Let loose of my mental load – all
my thoughts set free.
No problems of tomorrow, no
problems of today.
The problems now before me soon
will fade away.

BILL

He lowered his head
and played with his thumb.
In discomfort, sighed;
he acts rather glum.

Only fifty-four;
living in a home.
Always in a crowd;
he's always alone.

I told him I cared.
He looked up and grinned.
He lowered his head;
no talking begins.

This man only talks
of his physical pains.
He's going through life
with nothing to gain.

What can be done for
a man in this shape?
Can we engineer
confusion escape?

Our Children

Suicide used to be the final
weapon of the devastated.
A last effort to make a point;
a point still not made.
"I'll show them. They won't have
me to kick around any longer."

How misguided.

But now, the one so devastated has
taken aim on the decided cause
of their depression.
To abolish the youthful light
that surrounds them, before erasing
the hopeless flicker of their own.

How overwhelming.

One whose life span had been measured
in months not long before;
whose existence was the pure portrayal
of youthful beauty and endless dreams;
has now fallen into a psychological crevice
and can't survive the emotional implosion.

How little time.

We who claim to care,
must reach into the fire.
We must deliver our children again;
a re-birth; refuse their death.
The only hope our children have
is the hope we have within us.

How important.

When a child believes that their limited scope
represents the known boundaries of reality,
it's too easy for that child to
recklessly defend those boundaries
by seeking support from those whose
boundaries are apparently the same.

How unfortunate.

All too often, those whose
boundaries are alike
Do not allow for enough commonality
to overcome the barriers of entry.
The barriers become walls. Walls within
walls; known reality begins to implode.

How lonely.

The Wing of an Angel

(Song Lyric)

I fell to sleep one night
and began to dream of life.
A life so on the run;
then I only thought of one.
One who brought me joy;
who saw the man, not just the boy;
who stayed through the strife;
who agreed to be my wife.

Look at me, here I am,
standing on the wing of an Angel.
What I see, above the land,
an end to all the things I thought
    painful.
What a gift a man can have;
and for this gift I'll always be
    grateful.
Look at me, here I am,
standing on the wing of an Angel.

While on the Angel's wing I flew,
through the sky that was so blue,
I saw pictures of my past;
the good times and the bad.
She was always by my side,
keeping pace, stride for stride.
Fighting dragons in the day;
at night, by me she'd stay.

Look at me, here I am,
standing on the wing of an Angel.
What I see, above the land,
an end to all the things I thought painful.
What a gift a man can have;
and for this gift I'll always be grateful.
Look at me, here I am,
standing on the wing of an Angel.

As me dream went passed today
to a time still far away.
I could feel her loving smile
With its strength, mile after mile.
As we watched the setting Sun,
our own race was nearly done.
We had shared a love so real;
The Sandman could never steal.

Look at me, here I am,
standing on the wing of an Angel.
What I see, above the land,
an end to all the things I thought
    painful.
What a gift a man can have;
and for this gift I'll always be
    grateful.
Look at me, here I am,
standing on the wing of an Angel.

COME OUT AND PLAY

(Song Lyric)

I see this girl walkin' down the
    street.
Lookin' good,
From her head down to her feet.
She likes to wear her full mink
    coat;
with nothing else.
There's more that you should know.

You see her pearls glisten in the
    midnight glow.
She wears them proud;
and she likes to wear them low.
Later on, her pearls are in you
    hands.
She wears a smile,
as you reach the promise land.

The girl like to have a good time.
She likes to toy,
with your heart and with your mind.
When you meet her, you just want to say,
I'll be your boy.
Can Maxie come out and play?

There are times when you wonder who she is.
She seem to turn it up the later it gets.
But you know one thing when you're with this girl,
the excitement that she brings will rock your world.
Can Maxie come out and play?

The dance floor is where she wants to be.
A few sidecars and she has feathers for her feet.
She smiles as she asks you to dance.
You feel unsure, but decide to take a chance.

Once you're on the floor and lookin' in her eyes,
You know for sure if she left you'd want to die.
So you seize the moment the best you can.
You do your best to be Maxie's man.

With the moonlight shinin' in the car,
the top down;
and she wants to touch the stars.
You hear the tape playin' Rhapsody in Blue.
She's moving slow;
and she's movin' to the tune.

Maxie – The Ride Home

(Song Lyric)

I see Maxie, walking to her car.
She asks herself, Maxie, do you know who you are?
She wants to know who's in control of her life.
Is it the gangster's girl, or the gentleman's wife?

Only Maxie knows
What she wants more from this world.
Is it the woman she's become;
or, the unsatisfied girl?

As she's driving home, Maxie thinks about the day.
So many times throughout, she wanted to run away.
The radio is on, playing a lonesome song.
Giving it no thought, Maxie hums along.

Is it Maxie's turn
to break from the herd?
Or, will she remain,
feeling like a wounded bird?

As she turns the corner, Maxie is near her home.
Her husband's out tonight; Maxie's all alone.
Her mind drifts away to those times gone past.
Will she come to terms with her life at last?

Not even Maxie knows
where she'll go from here.
Will she find peace of mind;
or, will she shed a tear?
I see Maxie, walking from her car.

Oblivious

(Song Lyric)

I found myself on fire. Needed time to be alone.
Had to curb my desire; had a mind of its own.
The news hit me hard; knocked my feet from under me.
I heard the news from a friend. He helped the blind to see.

I had no stomach for the truth; no desire to hear the tale.
The girl was my life. I was not her only male.
With Pandora's Box now open, time for me to face the facts.
It doesn't matter what I do, I'll never get her back.

By the time I discovered, the news was growin' old.
She'd found another lover; our commitment now was cold.
It was a Hollywood secret; they all knew except for me.
I only have one answer, to how this thing can be.

I was oblivious.
I was oblivious.
Times I thought you loved me.
Times I thought you cared.
Times I thought I could trust you.
Times I thought we shared.
I was oblivious.
I was oblivious.

DIAMONDS AND JEANS

(Song Lyric)

We just got off the highway,
Been on the road for much too long.
Stopped in for a drink or two,
and to hear a country song.
A lot of ladies were dancin'.
The sight was pleasin' to our eyes.
Couldn't help but notice,
the lady's jewels as she danced by.

The song was over, she was thirsty;
and started walkin' towards the bar.
Starrin' at my partner;
We know how lucky we are.
This diamond-clad lady
walked between my friend and I.
without hesitation,
she seemed to know she caught our eyes.

She was movin' cross the dance floor;
The brightest eyes I'd ever seen.
More than a man could ask for,
In her diamonds and her jeans.

She said, "Good evening fellas.
The music is hot tonight.
Except for ridin' horses,
nothin' else can feel so right."
As she sipped her margarita,
my friend and I could see two things.
This girl was quite a lady,
And she wore a wedding ring.

Her diamonds were so striking;
she wore them like a queen.
She spoke often of her husband,
he didn't like the country scene.
She came here for the dancin'
and to hear a country song.
Wasn't looking for romancin'
to her husband that belongs.

The stranger said, "Good evenin' Baby,
may we share the next dance?"
He said, "I thought that maybe
I'd make my move while I had the chance."
She threw her arms around him,
then said, "My Love, I've missed you so.
I think that it's time
For my husband and me to go.

Her country boots were stompin' smoothly
as she'd glide around the room.
This southern girl was quite a beauty;
a yellow rose about to bloom.
She was movin' 'cross the dance floor;
the brightest eyes I'd ever seen.
More than a man could ask for,
in her diamonds and her jeans.

When this Yearbook was New

(Song Lyric)

What about the time,
when you and I were still young?
What about the time,
we thought tomorrow would never come?
What about the time,
when life was so new?
What about the time,
when this yearbook was new?

I was looking through an old yearbook.
Handwritten notes everywhere I looked.
I found your face in a picture there;
Same sweet smile with different hair.
Your note said to me, "My sweet boy,
Since meeting you I've known such joy.
The time we've shared is just the start.
Know this for sure, you have my heart."

I read the notes as the pages turned.
It seemed since then, so much I've learned.
One special note from your best friend,
"Boy if you're smart, your search should end.

She's a friend of mine, so I'll let you know
she dreams of you; she loves you so.
Life with her will be rich; her heart is true.
If you honor her, she'll treasure you."

I closed the book, laid it on the floor.
Tears in my eyes; I could take no more.
I have thoughts of you here in my arms.
I'd give everything to enjoy your charms.

It's still too fresh for me to understand
why I can't see you and hold your hand.
Just yesterday, you were laid to rest.
When you died, you took my best.

What about the time,
when you and I were
still young?
What about the time,
we thought tomorrow
would never come?
What about the time,
when life was so new?
What about the time,
before I lost you?
What about the time,
when this yearbook
was new?

AVENUES

Coming together as one
provides varied overtures
that all too often may stun
the unprotected heart.

Alger approaches set tones;
cutting, biting and caustic;
chill the soul beneath the bones
to isolate the heart.

Sugar is sweet and yet some
would say sugar makes you soft;
like soft smiles; like a Spring morn;
soft, like a tender heart.

When searching souls would converge,
tender pathways could be built
to allow a gentle merge –
richly filling the heart.

Warm the bridges of your love.
Make soft kisses a daily act.
Invite frivolous, soft hugs.
Embrace your lover's heart.

THIRD GRADE

Kid's play – kid's play,
run away – run away;
to that land where all kids play.
All the day, they play and play.

Night Dive

Dark gives way to the light's edge.
Pushed aside by the diver
who sought discovery by
immersing his frame well below
the veiled surface of the sea.

Not set apart by a wedge.
Hand held light and compressed life
offer the Terran access
to a vast world of vibrance;
wet with wonder – deep beneath.

It came from within the hold.
The creature lives in what once
carried dry Terrans between
surface ports of call; now still,
resting calm amid wet life.

Brightly jeweled lobster of old.
Shuffles across the metal
to avoid the diver's beam
aimed at the encrusted shell.
They only come out at night.

Enter the hold through the hull.
Inverse perception creates
wavy illusions of this
watery farm of sea life.
The ceiling is now the floor.

Move from room to room and mull
over the Terrans who filled
these spaces once brimming with air;
now wet, full of new life forms.
A Terran domain no more.

The Search

Love does not elude,

but it does give one a merry chase.

Ever within view,

softly nestled between time and space.

POISE

The head lifts –
positioning straight on the neck.
Eyes forward –
open, waiting to be met.

Shoulders back –
head tilted like classic art.
The lips curl –
a gentle view of the heart.

Voice escapes –
melodies flow from within.
Welcomed words –
new relationship begins.

Time eludes –
anxiousness gives way to peace.
Lovely poise –
mind, body, spirit complete.

Poetic Motion

Eyes actively search their field of vision.
Noting the expressions of all others.
Feelings are transmitted as the eyes lock.
A look that moves through the eyes to the heart.

Hands that reach warmly to pull others close;
caressing with a gentle tenderness.
Fingertips barely touch, but firmly hold.
Hands mold the pathway to finesse the heart.

Lips speak of love when they're silent.
They move, they curl; they entice the spirit.
Speaking soft words; murmuring pleasant sounds.
Kissing the skin lovingly lures the heart.

Legs are much more than vehicles of transport.
They encourage a man to conquer all.
They enlist the support of passersby.
Legs in motion give motion to the heart.

RED HOT MAMA

Statuesque, resting with a scorching look, yet no movement.
Demanding attention from eyes allowed the rewarding view.
Lines start with headlights and resolve through a rear spoiler.
Requiring touch, resisting nothing and promising all.
Once engaged, fluid movement barely allows restraint.
Smooth motion, responsive to the touch, purring slightly.
Restrained rumble; just the right pressure placed on the accelerator.
Pleasure replaces function; exhilaration overcomes thought.
On the journey, near dancing abounds; gentle rocking engulfs.
White-knuckling to the finish line.
Pushing through the incendiary moment.
One to one, two as one; Red Hot together.

Puppies

Any idea what goes through
those furry little heads?
Chasing each other across
over-stuffed chairs and beds.

Noises come from their insides –
smiling, growling, ranting;
falling over each other –
fun sounding like panting.

Anything's a toy – adventure;
to be rolled, chewed or chased.
Goals measured only loosely
by how paws and ears taste.

Puppies? No, woman and man.
Cool if it were but true.
Frolicking play; animal-like;
puppy-like – me and you.

THOUGHTS

Embracing this life;

    surviving Earth's gravity;

        blessed to have known you!

The fragile vail between realities

    looms reckless and permeable.

We fuel our creativity

    by whom we choose to surround ourselves.

THOUGHTS

The existential dichotomy between reality

    and wishful thinking, as seen on a Mesozoic plane,

        creates an unfathomable frustration which causes the need

            for further capitulation to arrive anywhere near resolution.

There's always a light at the end of the tunnel.

    If there's no light, maybe it's not a tunnel…

It was a mistake to come to this planet

    in the first place.

THOUGHTS

They say 'Ignorance is bliss.'

    Is it only blissful to the ignorant?

If you never give up,

    time is always on your side.

Fear cripples.

THOUGHTS

Patience –

    You either have it or you lose it.

Have you ever wondered why there are no absolutes?

    Could it be that we are 'always' the variables?

Whatever you do, do it like you mean it!

    Work like you mean it!

        Love like you mean it!

        Live like you mean it!

THOUGHTS

Hey, get your fingers

    off my buttons!

Is it better to change your circumstances,

    or acclimate to them?

She wants me to do cartwheels

    or something.

THOUGHTS

Your fear of short term failure

    can blind you to your long term success.

Are you becoming your enemy?

    Projection and assumption;

        evolving into what you hate;

            on a grand scale or just as an individual?

You have to Plan to Prevent.

THOUGHTS

Teach, don't tell.

    Educate, don't dictate.

Most often, people respond

    based on their various insecurities.

        How different relationships would be

            if people responded based on their strengths.

Feeling lost and out of sorts?

    Don't look down;

        keep your eyes on the horizon.

THOUGHTS

Such different levels of various friendships;

    nurtured differently and depended on in different manners.

Who they are often depends upon

    who you are.

You are the verses in my love song…

THOUGHTS

In life, like on the raging sea,

> when the winds threaten to knock you off your course,

> > or capsize you entirely,

> > > don't turn away – keep facin' it!

Five feet nothing, and worth the climb.

Been there, done that –

> refused the tee shirt.

THOUGHTS

It's better to walk into wall,

     than not open door at all…

Referring to the employed and those they provide service to –

     'Both sides of the time clock.'

Patience was never one of her vices…

THOUGHTS

Embrace the metaphor!

Love the view,

    or accept the dust.

If you're not pushing down buttons,

    you might be pushing up daisies.

THOUGHTS

Pay attention to the overwhelming beauty

of a single blade of grass.

S.E.E.Q.

Spherical Earth Epiphanies Quorum –

A group of currently Earth-bound individuals

recognizing the epiphanies of the past,

and seeking the epiphanies yet to come.

You must actively pursue your goals,

since the light at the end of the tunnel

is operated by a motion detector.

THOUGHTS

Whatever you do –

Be there when you do it!

Being Loved –

The magic of the heart, the grace of acceptance, and the wisdom, or luck, to know you're in it, embraces the Love given freely from sources all around.

Sometimes, it's not that what you are doing is Wrong…

It might be you just haven't done that one Right thing yet.

THOUGHTS

What is it like to truly see the world through another's eyes?

If looks could kill, you'd be a serial killer…

That dress owes you a big thank-you; 'cause you make it look good.

THOUGHTS

If you think you know it all, then that will be all you ever know.

The Road to Insanity may be treacherous, but it's short…

Quality and Success are not accidents – they are Forged!

The Mind of God

CHAPTER OUTLINE

CHAPTER ONE

We are a part of God – not separate

Chance are, life, as we know it, does not exist.

Consider for a moment a new, far-reaching theory, which fully engages pure, Christian faith in the one true God. A revolutionary theory that may stretch in ways you never thought possible the way we view God's existence as well as our own human existence and how the two relate closely to one another.

God is omniscient. How is it that God knows everything before it happens? God is omnipresent. How is it that God, as a Spirit, is everywhere at all times? God is omnipotent. How is it that God can work miracles that bypass all laws of physics and human understanding? I'm afraid to fully understand the answers to these and many other questions we'll need to wait until the day we can ask God directly; but until that day, I have a theory.

My theory is that we exist only in the Mind of God.

Yes, that's precisely what I said. Our entire human existence, from conception through and including our afterlife, may exist only within the realm of God's mind. Now, before you organize a group of angry and powerful vigilantes to quickly light the all-consuming fires of Hell and burn my soon-to-be questionable 'existence' to an indiscernible crisp, this theory is not at all intended to lesson or in any other way diminish the elements of a comforting and valued Christian faith. Quite the contrary, this newly postulated theory is presented as another human effort to continue to understand the oft spoken of and nowhere nearly comprehended Mind of God.

From what we have been taught throughout the numbered years of our extensive religious teachings, God is accepted as some unseen, indescribable form of spiritual being or existence well beyond our limited understanding. As an example, there's the whole theological teaching of the Holy Trinity where God the Father, Jesus Christ His Son, and the Holy Spirit are inexplicably one in the same. I believe this fully, by my faith in God, with no hesitation or doubt. But, if we were to apply the various faith-based, non-provable issues that directly relate to the Holy Trinity against this newly asserted and strangely empowering theory that we all exist only within the Mind of God, I believe we can have a better understanding of how the Holy Trinity can be exactly and precisely what it has been taught to us to be.

Looking for a moment at a few insightful aspects of our relationship with God may help introduce this theory. I believe, and many others do as well, that God is both our Creator and Father. From the early writings of Christian faith, this postulate was viewed as a foundation of our faith.

Irenaeus, an early defender of the faith, lived and wrote of his beliefs during the years of 130 AD and 202 AD. Irenaeus was considered quite enlightened in the thinking and application of Christian elements of faith as well as with overall theological aspects of a true belief in God. In his work addressing God as both Creator and Father, he states, "The rule of truth we hold is, that there is one God Almighty, who made all things by His Word, and fashioned and formed that which has existence out of that which has none, there is no exception; but the Father made all things by Him, both visible and invisible, objects by angels or by any powers separated from His thought." (Pages 29-30, Readings in Christian Thought)

These are writings both in scripture and from numerous defenders of the faith that speak of and work to describe the existence of God and thus the existence of mankind within the realm of God. Looking at these and allowing our minds to realize that we cannot come close to the understanding and discovering the totality of God, should allow us to open our human imaginations just enough to explore this new theory that our complete existence is within the thoughts and imagination of God. To better understand one's father is to grow much closer to him.

Now, there will be those who feel or believe that this theory somehow diminishes the importance of our existence. To them I point out that to limit the scriptural importance of our existence within the Mind of God is to limit God Himself. Further, they may feel that our role within God's plan is somehow insignificant if in fact we dwell within the Mind of God. To that point I assert that to downplay our role within the Mind of God is to doubt the relevance of God's plan and all that God offers to us, His children, born of Him alone.

So, there you have it. The basic premise of this new, exciting theory. Let us now introduce a few parameters of thinking to use as we begin to examine the possibility that this theory is more than a theory – the possibility that the elements of this theory are true and worthy of acceptance.

CHAPTER TWO

Religion and Theology

In order to begin a studious examination of this theory. It's important to take a close look at a few definitions and concepts. The first and foremost is the term *religion*. Let's first address how religion is defined academically. Academically, religion can be defined with at least four description, each with subtle variations.

1. Creator: "Belief in and reverence for a supernatural power or powers regarded as creator or governor of the universe." (American Heritage College Dictionary, 1997 – AHCD, 97)
2. Spiritual leader: "A set of beliefs, values, and practices based on the teachings of a spiritual leader." (AHCD, 97)
3. Cause: "A cause, principle, or an activity pursued with zeal or conscientious devotion." (AHCD, 97)
4. Influence for good: "To accept a higher power as a controlling influence for the good in one's life." (AHCD, 97)

Creator: What is it about religion that feeds the human emotions? As defined above, religion is first a system of beliefs in the Creator of the universe. Seems simple enough, but there are many who feel that nature was the creator of all that is known. Evolution and the Big Bang are just a couple of explanations for some people.

One who believes that God is the Creator of the universe, an all else for that matter, can accept that theories such as Evolution and the Big Bang may in fact be processes used by God as He created all that is known.

Spiritual Leader: Second, religion focuses on the teachings of a spiritual leader. These teachings can vary from those of Jesus, Muhammad, Buddha or Jim Jones. A spiritual leader can also use the teachings of their spiritual leader to lead others into alternate life styles. A tie or connection to a spiritual leader is a very emotional consideration. To sacrifice one's life for the life, or more specifically in this case, the teachings of another is viewed as the ultimate example of total devotion.

Cause: One need only look at the results of members of a religious sect who followed the teachings and guidance of their leader to cause the crashing of airplanes into buildings taking the lives of seemingly unrelated individuals in the name of their religion and its cause. Not isolated to modern day events, Cause has been a reason for many religious extremes such as the Holy Wars of early England or the taking of the Holy Land by the Israelites.

Influence for good: There are certainly those who see their religion centered on a force that brings good into their lives. This higher power is given credit for the benefits, gifts, treasures and all other applicable occurrences within one's life.

What does this say about religion? It says that religion is a matter of the heart. Religion does not need to be faced on any facts or specific truths if there is sufficient faith in either the Creator, the Spiritual Leader, the Cause, the Influence for good or any combination of these elements. One does not easily argue religion. Religion is so deeply based on emotional elements that an immediate defensiveness arise in the hearts and spirits of the believer.

As we begin to examine the Mind of God theory, another term we should examine is what theory is. Theory is defined as the "Systematically organized knowledge applicable in a wide variety of circumstances…Abstract reasoning; speculation; a conjecture; an assumption based on limited information or knowledge." (AHCD. 97)

When looking at any theory, especially one that deals with the Almighty, the examiner must keep in mind that feathers may be ruffled if the postulates are inferred in a manner they were never intended to imply. Thus, understanding the elements of a theory are important reminders of the focus of research and assumption.

A third definition, and probably the most detailed, is the meaning behind Theology. The AHCD, 97, defines theology as, "1. The study of the nature of God and religious truth. 2. A system or school of opinions concerning God and religious questions. 3. A course of specialized study usually at a college or seminary."

The study of the nature of God; opinions concerning God; questions; specialized study; theology looks at the elements of the belief in God in such a manner that seeks to define and in fact refine a deeper understanding of the Almighty and His plan.

Theology should be presented in a manner that is understandable. It does no good to present information if no one understands no matter how important or valuable it may be. Theology requires detailed explanation that works to lead the seeker to an open-minded view of the theory being presented. Theology by its very nature is the study of the elements of God and thus is based primarily on the Bible. When other sources are used to examine a God-related theory, they should never be found to argue with or attempt to confound the Bible. If they do, their validity within a theological study is highly devalued.

There are methods of theological study that differ in their approaches and intents. A brief look at a few of these methods will help us with our examination of the theory of the Mind of God. These are:

- Biblical Theology: Biblical Theology uses the Bible as its ultimate source material. It pays attention to biblical history and the climate and conditions of the times of those writing and receiving the histories. Biblical Theology recognizes that the recorded revelations came about as a result of progressive stages of the lives and events experienced by a variety of individuals.

- Systematic Theology: Systematic Theology coordinates and organizes variety of information of biblical revelations, historical backgrounds, scholarly commentary and other valid source materials in an organized effort to focus on the total structure of biblical truth.
- Historical Theology: The Historical Theology method focuses on others who have studied the Bible and its teachings and then made their own determinations as to the outcomes of their studies. Many of these determinations could be looked at as decisions based on the precedents set by earlier church fathers and teachings. Many doctrines are derived from this method of study.

There are certainly other methods and approaches for theological study, but these are the methods chosen for this theory. They meet the tests of biblical validity and they honor and cherish a rich and fruitful relationship with our Lord.

How does religion and theology relate? Let's take a look at the correlation of these two valuable and interwoven elements from a slightly different perspective than may be usually taken. Let's look at these two elements from the point of view of needs – our need for religion and our corresponding need for theology.

Phil Ford

In the field of Social Psychology, a modern social scientist, Abraham Maslow, structured a theory of the varied needs of individuals and the satisfaction of those needs. Maslow separated various needs into two groups. He labeled those needs as Basic Needs and Meta-needs. (Understanding Human Behavior, p. 630) Maslow looked at the Basic Needs as life sustaining drives and the Meta-needs as growth and enrichment needs.

Within those needs identified by Maslow as basic needs, individual needs such as hunger, thirst, affection, sex, security and esteem exist. According to Maslow, an individual must have those needs satisfied merely to sustain life and that if any of these needs are not satisfied, then moving on to satisfy the Meta or growth needs becomes difficult or even impossible.

Meta or growth needs consist of the appreciation of beauty, achieving order, working for and in unity with others, seeking, fighting for and acquiring justice and relishing and nurturing goodness. Both sets of needs described within these pages could be detailed in much greater depth if this were a treatise examining elements within Social Psychology. But, for the purposes of this study, this explanation should suffice.

It is my assumption that religion and theology relate to one another as Maslow's life sustaining and growth needs relate to one another. In religion, one finds the basic needs of faith addressed and satisfied. One finds in religion the acceptance of God, our Creator, as the supernatural power of the universe. One finds spiritual leadership in Jesus Christ and the profits of the Old and New Testaments to help establish a set of beliefs and values. An individual with a chosen religion can claim a cause to work for with all the zeal and devotion they can muster. Finally, when one has accepted a course of religion, they have a wondrous higher power to praise for the good that comes to that individual's life through the faith and belief of the religion.

Taking the next step with our look at the correlation between religion and theology, one finds in theology the efforts to satisfy the Meta or growth needs of our faith. The need to know more about the who, what, when, where, why and how of our beliefs. By seeking to satisfy our growth needs, we search out the deeper meanings behind the powerful and meaningful histories, parables and descriptions given to us through revelation in the Bible. We may not truly know or understand God's fullness of thought and intent in any of our beliefs until the day we sit in His throne room and have the rich opportunity to ask Him the question directly in a time and place where the fullness of the answer can be understood. But our desire to know our Father as well as we humanly can drives us beyond the satisfaction of our basic need for religion and pushes us toward a study of the depth of the spiritual issues to attempt to satisfy some of our growth needs.

Religion is a matter of the heart – the satisfaction of our basic needs for our belief in God and our salvation. Religion is not something argued between believers. It is accepted and cherished. Theology on the other hand, can be argued all day long. In fact, it is most often the argument that helps to nourish the growth of the theological issue to a level of intellectual acceptance. If we are wrong about our religion, that carries significant ramifications; whereas, if we are wrong about our theology our basic needs of faith are left undamaged, sound and solid, carrying us on within our relationship with God.

Chapter Three

Testing the Theory

To begin testing our theory of the Mind of God, we should look first to the Summa Theologica (The Theological Sum) and its author and architect, Thomas Aquinas, for help. Aquinas (1225 - 1274 AD), known even during his life as the Architect of Systematic Theology, created a standard for theologians to follow and a level of aptitude to strive towards. It has been said that cathedrals were built of solid stone but that Thomas Aquinas built the theological system of enduring ideas.

Thomas Aquinas was born in the town of Aquino, which rests between Rome and Naples, Italy. After completing his studies in Cologne and Paris, Aquinas lectured in Rome, Bologna, Pisa and Naples. Aquinas was seen as a systematic thinker and writer with a neat, orderly mind that delighted in logical and dialectical endeavors. Aquinas often references the work of one of his theological predecessors, Augustine. Additional important influence in the works that relate to our work here come from Aquinas' being greatly influenced by the precision of definition and syllogistic distinction in philosophical and theological construction of thought provided by the philosopher, Aristotle. Aquinas so often refers to Aristotle merely as "The Philosopher" as he does in his Third Article of Whether God Exists?

Aquinas writes his treatise testing whether God exists using his chosen five ways. It is the intent of this treatise of the theory of the Mind of God to use the same five ways to address the Essence of God that Aquinas uses in testing the Existence of God. To do so, we must first look at Aquinas' Third Article in its entirety to see how he exercises the five ways and then apply them to this current test.

THIRD ARTICLE: Whether God exists?
We proceed thus to the Third Article:

Objection 1. It seems that God does not exist; because if one of two contraries be infinite, the other would be altogether destroyed. But the word "God" means that He is infinite goodness. If, therefore, God existed, there would be no evil discoverable; but there is evil in the world. Therefore God does not exist.

Objection 2. Further, it is superfluous to suppose that what can be accounted for by a few principles has been produced by many. But it seems that everything we see in the world can be accounted for by other principles, supposing God did not exist. For all natural things can be reduced to one principle, which is human reason, or will. Therefore there is no need to suppose God's existence.

On the contrary, It is said in the person of God: "I am Who I am" (Exodus 3:14). *I answer that*, The existence of God can be proved in five ways. The first and more manifest way is the argument from motion. It is certain, and evident to our senses, that in the world some things are in motion. Now whatever is in motion is put into motion by another, for nothing can be in motion except it is in potentiality to that towards which it is on motion; whereas a thing moves inasmuch as it is in act. For motion is nothing else than a reduction of something from potentiality to actuality. But nothing can be reduced from potentiality to actuality, except by something in a state of actuality. Thus that which is actually hot, as fire, makes wood, which is potentially hot, to be actually hot, and thereby move and changes it. Now it is not possible that the same thing should be at once in actuality and potentiality in the same respect, but only in different respects. For what is actually hot cannot simultaneously be potentially hot; but it is simultaneously potentially cold. It is therefore impossible that in the same respect and in the same way a thing should be both mover and moved, i.e., that it should move itself. Therefore, whatever is in motion must have been put in motion, then this also must needs be put in motion by another, and that by another again. But this cannot go on to infinity, because then there would be no first mover, and, consequently, no other mover; seeing that subsequent movers move only inasmuch as they are put in motion by the first mover; as the staff moves only because it is put in motion by the hand. Therefore it is necessary to arrive at a first mover, put in motion by no other, and this everyone understands to be God.

The second way if from the nature of the efficient cause. In the world of sense we find there is an order of efficient causes. There is no case known (neither is it, indeed, possible) in which a thing is found to be the efficient cause of itself; for so it would be prior to itself, which is impossible. Now in efficient causes it is not possible to go on to infinity, because in all efficient causes following order, the first is the cause of the intermediate cause, and the intermediate is the cause of the ultimate cause, whether the intermediate cause be several, or one only. Now to take away the cause is to take away the effect. Therefore, if there be no first cause among efficient causes, there will be no ultimate, nor any intermediate cause. But if in efficient causes it is possible to go to infinity, there will be no first efficient cause, neither will there be an ultimate effect, nor any intermediate efficient causes; all of which is plainly false. Therefore it is necessary to admit a first efficient cause, to which everyone gives the name of God.

The third way is taken from possibility and necessity, and runs thus. We find in nature things that are possible to be and not to be, since they are found to be generated, and to be corrupted, and consequently, they are possible to be and not to be. But it is impossible for these always exist, for that which is possible not to be at the same time is not. Therefore, if everything is possible not to be, then at one time there could have been nothing in existence. Now if this were true, even now there would be nothing in existence, because that which does not exist only begins by something already existing. Therefore, if at one time nothing was in existence, it would have been impossible for anything to have begun to exist; and thus even now nothing would be in existence – which is absurd. Therefore, not all beings are merely possible, but there must exist something the existence of which is necessary. But every necessary thing either has its necessity caused by another, or not. Now it is impossible to go on to infinity in necessary things which have their necessity caused by another, as has been already proved in regard to efficient causes. Therefore we cannot but postulate the existence of some being having of itself its own necessity, and not receiving it from another, but rather causing in others their necessity. This all men speak if as God.

The fourth way is taken from the graduation to be found in things. Among beings there are some more and some less good, true, noble, and the like. But "more" and "less" are predicated of different things, according as they resemble in their different ways something which is maximum, as a thing is said to be hotter according as it more nearly resembles that which is hottest; so that there is something which is truest, something best, something noblest, and consequently, something which is uttermost being; for those things that are greatest in being, as it is written in (Aristotle's) De Metaphysica, ii. Now the maximum is any genus is the cause of all in that genus; as fire, which is the maximum of heat, is the cause of all hot things. Therefore there must also be something which is to all beings the cause of their being, goodness, and every other perfection; and this we call God.

The fifth way is taken from the governance of the world. We see that things which lack intelligence, such as natural bodies, act for an end, and this is evident from their acting always, or nearly always, in the same way, so as to obtain the best result. Hence it is plain that not fortuitously, but designedly, do they achieve their end. Now whatever lacks intelligence cannot move towards an end, unless it be directed by some being endowed with knowledge and intelligence; as the arrow is shot to its mark by the archer. Therefore some intelligent beings exist by whom all natural things are directed to their end; and this being we call God.

Reply Objection 1. As Augustine says (Enchiridion, xi): "Since God is the highest good, He would not allow any evil in His works, unless His omnipotence and goodness were such as to bring good even out of evil." This is part of the infinite goodness of God, which He should allow evil to exist, and out of it produce good.

Reply Objection2. Since nature works for a determinate end under the direction of a higher agent, whatever is done by nature must needs be traced back to God, as to it first cause. So also whatever is done voluntarily must also be traced back to some higher cause than human reason or will, since these can change and fail; for all things that are changeable and capable of defect must be traced back to an immovable and self-necessary first principle, as we shown in the body of the Article.

Reviewing the words of Aquinas can be revealing and at times overwhelming in its complicated simplicity. But to do so allows for man's reason to attack such normally faith-based questions as the existence of God and the Mind of God. Aquinas helps us again by stating in his second article, "...for the question of essence follows on the question of existence."

To summarize, Aquinas utilizes five ways to test the existence of God: (Quoted from Aquinas' Third Article)

1. Motion:
   "Therefore it is necessary to arrive at a firs mover, put into motion by no other; and this everyone understands to be God."

2. Efficient Cause:
   "Therefore, if there be no first cause among efficient causes, there will be no ultimate, nor any intermediate cause. Therefore it is necessary to admit a first efficient cause, to which everyone gives the name of God."

3. Possibility and Necessity:

"Therefore we cannot but postulate the existence of some being having if itself its own necessity, and not receiving it from another, but rather causing in others their necessity. This all men speak of as God."

4. Gradation to be found in things:
"Therefore there must also be something which is to all things the cause of their being, goodness, and every other perfection; and this we call God."

5. Governance of the World:
"Therefore some intelligent being exists by whom all natural things are directed to their end; and this being we call God."

As Aquinas said, the question of essence follows the question of existence, so let's incorporate these five ways that Aquinas has used to prove the existence of God to attempt to prove a possible Essence of God.

The first way: Motion.

God exists as the first mover as is described by Aquinas.

God breathed life into man.

God gave man actuality where only potentiality existed before God's motion on man.

God sharing His Essence generated man.

God spoke and man became; God *thought* and man existed for the first time.

Therefore, since God, through the motion of being the first mover, gave actuality to man by thinking man into existence, therefore man was created within the thoughts of God; within the Mind of God.

Since God moved through His thought and caused man to exist and thus have thought of his own, this action caused an effect, as a result of efficient cause, resulting in the thoughts of all mankind. Therefore, mankind could have no thought had not God first moved through efficient cause to use His own thought to give life to thought within mankind. God's thought, the efficient cause, gave life to mankind within the Mind of God.

The third way: Possibility and necessity.

God's essence is necessary for the existence of man's essence. The essence of mankind is a possibility that without the necessity of God's essence could not exist. Man's essence has a finite nature to it, thus according to Aquinas at one time did not exist. Therefore, at one time, man had no essence and it was only through God's Essence of Thought that the first motion of God by which the use of His efficient cause generated an effect that sprung from His necessity that the possibility of man's essence became a reality.

The fourth way: Gradation to be found in things.

This fourth way looks to be the good that is found in all things and grants the genus of that goodness to the maximum goodness, God. In comparing the Mind of God theory to the gradation to be found in all things, one can see that the thoughts that man has that are good must then originate from God. It is thus the good thoughts that man has that leads man to do good within his own existence. Therefore, the good thoughts of man originate from God's own thoughts, which then lead us to accept that our very goodness residents within the thoughts or Mind of God.

The fifth way: Governance of the World.

The fifth and final way Aquinas has used addresses the intelligence and knowledge of God. It is the intelligence and knowledge of God that moves, through design, towards an end. Thus, the proof of the existence of God gives the power of God to God's intelligence and knowledge. Therefore, it is God's intelligence and knowledge, easily accepted as primary elements of the Mind of God, which are naturally a portion of the true essence of God.

To summarize, using Aquinas' five ways of proving a theory relating to God, we find that the Mind of God can be shown as follows:

1. God's Essence of Thought (Mind of God) was the first motion.
2. Through efficient cause God used His own thought (Mind of God) to give life to thought within mankind.
3. It is only from the necessity of the Mind of God that the possibility of man's essence became a reality.

4. Our very goodness resides within our thoughts or the Mind of God.
5. God's intelligence and His knowledge, primary elements of the Mind of God, are elements that are a natural portion of the true Essence of God.

Chapter Four

Correlation of Our Beliefs

As we continue to examine the theory that we may exist only within the Mind of God, there are several elements believers look to as key elements or topics important to their faith. Let's briefly examine four of these elements. They are:

1. Faith
2. Sin
3. Christ, our Lord
4. Salvation

Faith: Faith is the very basis for spiritual connection. Faith is defined in the Bible as "the proof of things hoped for; the evidence of things not seen" (KLV, Hebrews 11:1). What is our faith based on? Isn't our faith based on the existence of a loving and caring Creator / Father whom we can go to through prayer and who has promised that He is always with us?

How does this view of our faith correlate with our Mind of God theory? It correlates very well. By accepting that God is our Creator / Father whom we believe listens as we pray, the form that He exists in or within does not alter our faith. God is what he is – He is the great 'I am' of the Old Testament. It's not His form that makes Him what He is. It is His acts and fulfilled promises that effect the faith that we have in Him.

Sin: Sin has many definitions and many resulting after effects. It is often spoken as if a person sins against another person. This is partially true since the person feels the initial resulting effect of being sinned against. But there is a deeper and more fundamental root to the definition of sin.

Sin is action directly against God. The essence of sin is to go against the teaching and directives of God. The first sin, eating from the Tree of Knowledge of Good and Evil in the Garden of Eden, was against a specific directive of God. Neither Adam nor Eve knew the why behind the directive, but they knew it was God's wishes that they not take fruit from that specific tree.

So, in relation to the Mind of God theory, sin is sin no matter the form of God's essence. His teachings and directives are the same no matter His form. To sin against God is just what it is.

Christ, our Lord: Our dear Lord, Jesus, is the Son of God and our Savior. He came to Earth and lived with us as one of us; was tortured and put to death by methods known to man as most extreme. This reality that we know as our life is what Christ accepted as His own reality for a time. Whatever this reality is, in it we humans know the potential for pain on many levels. Chris, our Lord and Savior, accepted the full and un-buffered existence of this life on Earth as the essence of His great sacrifice for each and every one of us experiencing the onslaught of emotions – both good and bad – to best understand and show the magnitude of His sacrifice. The life and death of Christ was an example to mankind of the many, many attributes God desires for us to employ. (Matthew 20:28; 26:28)

Not fully understanding, and not pretending to either, how we yet fit into the Mind of God theory, it is most apparently clear that Christ lived as we live and died as we die. Nothing is taken away from the sacrifice that Christ made for us by accepting the Mind of God theory since we would also continue to accept every word of the Bible that Christ came to our existence through a miracle of birth and lived and died as we do.

Salvation: Salvation first goes hand in hand with our belief in Christ, whether we accept the Mind of God theory or not. Salvation goes further though. Salvation embraces all rime – past, present and future. It relates to all mankind. Salvation looks to God's love, His Grace and His Example to and for His Creation, us. To continue within the Grace of God is to continue to commune with God. This continued relationship with our Creator / Father is provided to us as a result of the Love of God and would be present no matter the form or essence of God's being. Accepting this as truth allows us to view the existence of God in any way we theologically choose without detracting from the wonder of God and the gift of His Salvation.

Chapter Five

What is Reality?

Before we move to pull all of the pieces together, I feel it would be beneficial to add one more discussion to the mix, which might be used as a barometer of critical thinking. What is reality?

Reality, as defined by 1993 American Heritage College Dictionary, is:

1. "The quality or state of being actual or true;
2. One, such as a person or an event, that is actual;
3. The totality of all things possessing actuality, existence, or essence;
4. That which exists objectively and in fact;
5. That which has necessary and not contingent existence."

Reading the elements of the definition of reality and then weaving some or all of those elements into a concept of what our reality of existence is can be seen first as evident. The third part of the definition addresses this when it reads that reality is the "totality of all things possessing actuality, existence or essence." We see our existence in the universe as possessing these elements, those of actuality and essence. We directly and indirectly test those elements each day of our existence.

To take this definition of reality and measure our proposed existence within the Mind of God against it poses no argument. Our reality, perceived or actual, rests as the 'quality or state of being actual or true.' We as mankind make a determination of what we view as actual or true. We make a science of testing these measurements with other tools of our own design.

What is the reality of God? Since God is overwhelmingly different from us, how can we fathom the reality of God? We try, and try we must since we hunger to know more about our Lord, to seek a deeper understanding of what is reality to God. God sought to understand our reality better by having Christ live and die within our reality.

What's the point in addressing reality at this juncture? The point is that we are not able to understand the vast nature of the reality of God and since we cannot, we must guard against limiting our understanding of God's reality to our human understanding.

CHAPTER SIX

Tie it all Together

We accepted that God is omniscient, omnipotent and omnipresent. We then postulated the theory that our entire human existence, from conception through and including our afterlife, may exist only within the realm of God's Mind.

To examine this theory we looked at the differences between religion, that matter of the heart, and theology, an in-depth study of what we are, why we're here and how we relate to our Creator / Father. We then moved to establish reasoning for the need to examine theology for a deeper understanding of our Father looking at the differences between basic needs and growth needs as described by Abraham Maslow.

We laid the groundwork for a valid study by looking at the varied study methods of Biblical Theology (The Bible as the ultimate source), Systemic Theology (Coordinating a variety of sources to focus on biblical truth), and Historical Theology (Determinations based on research precedents).

It was the enlightened work of Thomas Aquinas that was used to test the theory through his five ways of:

1. Motion: God's Essence of Thought (Mind of God) was the first motion.

2. Efficient Cause: Through efficient cause God used His own thought (Mind of God) to give life to thought within mankind.

3. Possibility and necessity: It is only from the necessity of the Mind of God that the possibility of man's essence became a reality.

4. Gradation to be found in things: Our very goodness resides within the thoughts or the Mind of God.

5. Governance of the World: God's intelligence and His knowledge, primary elements of the Mind of God, are elements that are a natural portion of the true Essence of God.

We moved on to look at a few of the elements of our faith: faith, sin, Christ, and salvation and how they correlate to this theory.

Through the diligent use of these methods and the functional nature of the material, it has been clearly shown that it is quite possible that we do exist within the Mind of God.

Chapter Seven

We are Empowered

Knowing that we are residents of the Mind of God empowers us.

- It gives credence that we are always connected to God and as such He hears us immediately. Being connected in this manner give us power and authority as described in the Bible.
- This explains how God knows our thoughts since our thoughts are a part of His thoughts.
- The act and process of prayer is given identifiable substance as a method of communicating with God.
- It qualifies and validates our faith in God's omniscience, omnipresence and omnipotence.
- It explains the events of honestly expressed psychic powers that some people have the ability to exercise. Their thoughts are in specific ways 'in line' with a piece of the Mind of God that allows them to 'tap in' to the omnipresence and omniscience of God allowing them to see or know things that appear to have been discovered through supernatural methods.

These are only a few of the ways we can be empowered by understanding this connected relationship with our Lord. Our expanded view of our Father and Creator through the acceptance of being a part of the Mind of God brings us closer and truly establishes us as a part of God.

As with any aspect of our wonderful relationship with God, the stronger that relationship, the stronger our relationships are with those whom we share this world. The scripture is quite clear that if we say we love and are connected with God then we must love and be connected with people. These two relationships are one in the same in their strength of connection. We are thus further empowered by being closer to our brothers and sisters through a closer connection with our Father.

Taking into account all that has been stated and examined throughout this study, it should be evident that our daily walk with God can be better understood and further enriched through the knowledge and exercise of that knowledge that we are an actual part of the Mind of God.

List of References used in the contemplation and construction of this theory:

1. *The Holy Bible* – King James
2. *The Holy Bible* – New International Version
3. *Commentary on the Whole Bible*, Matthew Henry
4. *Wycliffe Commentary*
5. *Basic Theology*, Charles C. Ryrie
6. *Readings in Christian Thought*, Hugh T. Kerr
7. *New Testament Survey*, Merrill C. Tenney
8. *Christian Thought-Volume Two*, Albert F. Gray
9. *Jesus in History*, Howard Clark Kee
10. *Nave's Topical Bible*
11. *Strong's Greek-Hebrew Dictionary*
12. *Thayer's Greek Definitions*
13. *Understanding Human Behavior*, James V. McConnell
14. *American Heritage College Dictionary, Houghton, Mifflin Company, Third Edition, 1997*

Printed in the United States
By Bookmasters